To margie
with love
from Shshn

S0-BIR-350

Not God After All

Not God After All

Gerald Stern

drawings by
Sheba Sharrow

Autumn House
Press

"Autumn House" and "Autumn House Press" are registered trade-
marks owned by Autumn House Press, a non-profit corporation
whose mission is the publication and promotion of poetry.

Text and cover design: Kathy Boykowycz
Cover painting: Sheba Sharrow

Autumn House Press
Editor: Michael Simms
Director of Development: Susan Hutton
Community Outreach Director: Michael Wurster
Assistant Editor: Jack Wolford
Editorial Consultant: Eva Simms
Media Consultant: Jan Beatty
Marketing Consultant: Matt Hamman

Printed in the USA by Thomson-Shore of Dexter, Michigan

All Autumn House books are printed on acid free paper and meet
the international standards for permanent books intended for pur-
chase by libraries.

ISBN 1-932870-02-4
Library of Congress Control Number: 2004109712

The Autumn House Poetry Series

Michael Simms, editor

Introduction

These aphorisms, petite narratives, whatever they are, were written over a period of two weeks in the Spring of 2002. They represent my feelings during that time, feelings that were angry, arch, focused, political, and unified. They also reflect both my reading and the sheer accident of my experience.

They constitute a narrative of a particular journey and a "conversation" I was having then, in both cases both literal and figurative. They are a little ruthless. They comprise both the intellectual and the pop, sometimes simultaneously, and of course reflect my interest, my knowledge and my prejudice, such as they are. If they light, say, on the character of Pétain, it is only that I was thinking about him, and hating him, and holding him accountable.

There are idioms, Yiddishisms, and solipsisms. There is reference to a trip my love Anne Marie and I took to Puerto Rico during that two week period. There is an extended reference to Odysseus's love of Nausicaa, the age difference between them and his betrayal of her, at least his coldness and evasions; and there is an extended reference to the Israelites, out of Exodus, as slaves and bricklayers. Along the way there is mention of boxers, singers, comedians, writers, presidents, wines, dogs, lovers, and friends.

They are presented more or less in the order written. They may constitute a more logical and aesthetically satisfying whole than I realize, even if that whole is merely one slice of time. They are also, as all writing is, a record of that time, only perhaps more so, and they are meant to give pleasure, at the very least that.

As far as the music, they respond to the song that was in my mind—and my job was to remember the words. As far as the form, each stanza has two lines and the two lines together constitute fourteen syllables, my counting. I wasn't imitating anything or anyone but, along the way, I did think of Proverbs, and Chinese and Japanese and Roman poetry, Juvenal especially, though I like to think of myself as kinder than that great poet, less involved in grudges.

If there is anything I agonize over, it's the difficulty of reference, but what could I do? Saul Bellow's camel hair overcoat I saw one cold day under the El in Chicago, when we passed each other, both of us knowing something, neither of us stopping. Ike Williams, the greatest lightweight of modern time, did spend an evening with me in Dunkin Donuts—in Highland Park, New Jersey—showing me the huge scrapbook he carried with him. He was on his way to teach boxing to boys for four dollars an hour. "Chicago Semite Viennese"? A line from Eliot. Dolgapyat? My family name before we moved to America.

It would have been nice maybe to write 500 of these, or 5,000, rather than 228, but I did what I wanted to do. We live in a wretched time, Hayden Carruth says, and I'm frankly a little surprised I wasn't less loving when I stripped down. Our job, for a long time to come, is to decide what to do about the whip, ignore it, embrace it, deny it, transform it, explain it. I wish everyone joy.

Gerald Stern

I don't know what the color
of the iris first was, blue?

■

For my immortality
I wear only purple socks.

■

Down with Rome, except for
Catullus, Ovid, etc.

■

Not one philosopher in
a thousand years, not one song.

■

A beaver eating loosestrife,
none of us could believe it.

■

It's all about family, my
ass, it's about money.

■

The sad thing is that when I
leave it will be the same thing.

■

I will be back with the
poison in less than an hour.

■

What is visible, what is
invisible, the same thing?

■

I'll never forget him,
especially since we didn't speak.

■

The beaver was mine to begin
with (she should know, shouldn't she?)

■

I'll never forget Saul Bellow's
camel-hair overcoat.

■

He played the clarinet with
twenty fingers on each hand.

■

On the whole I'd rather be
in Lambertville, New Jersey.

■

Reading Gombrowicz in Puerto
Rico—speaking Polish.

■

The gloom of the county fair—
most of all the white diesels.

■

On the whole, I'd prefer Iowa
City, Iowa.

■

Sweaters, boots, skates, scarves, hats, gloves,
books, sleds, salt, sand, wintershit.

■

On the whole wouldn't you rather
be in Philadelphia?

■

Where did you stay last night, there
was a white swan in my bed.

■

The Jesuits ah, the Jesuits
ah, the question Joosh.

■

Don't make God come too fast, be
a bastard a while longer.

■

A fire I understand,
but how do you make a flood?

■

Numero Uno, the name
of our hotel in San Juan.

■

Just like flies all over the place,
they're good workers though.

■

They run around the roof like
ants, play football during lunch.

■

Talk about the mother of
the bride, talk about black flies.

■

I'm ashamed of being an
American, him in the bushes.

■

I was glad to be born in
a place where Jews weren't lined up.

■

Galen was my first doctor,
a pediatrician.

■

The reckless affection of
her unconditional love.

■

Have you begun to shrink yet?
Are you getting smaller?

■

What kind of géneral was
le maréchal, old piss-face?

■

Liberté, égalité,
fraternité, same bullshit.

■

Just one hour or two,
depending on the locality.

■

The Pétain regime passed its
own Statut des Juifs.

■

James Farmer, John L. Lewis—
I know you have no idea.

■

Talk about black flies, talk
about photographers.

■

Who runs the mother's
funeral, the son or the rabbi?

■

The fat president ate his
oysters on slivers of ice.

■

How his love scolded him and
his psychiatrist pitched in.

■

The poem about me is the
best poem you ever wrote.

■

Long term economic problems—
trust the Republicans.

■

How I drowned my love at
Numero Uno in San Juan.

■

Pétain and his ministers
collaborated fully.

■

They were prepared, the trains
began to roll east in July.

■

Zola, Zola, my
Bulgarian Jew, my Moroccan.

■

The Shit Out of Luck Blues,
Weary Blues, Potato Skin Blues.

■

There is a plaque for Wendell
Wilkie on Fortieth Street.

■

Judy was a friend of mine—
she could do it any time.

■

The two lions guarding
our library are genderless.

■

I made a speech for Adlai
Stevenson on Market Street.

■

The garland briefer than a
girl's—unbelievable line.

■

The cat rubbing up against
me is an adolescent.

■

Small coconut—not throwing
it at the pigeons—old age.

■

A palm tree has finally
wrapped itself around my heart.

■

I judge everyone by
the length of her fingers—sorry!

■

What a life with women, I'm
just now thinking it over.

■

My daughters, my ducats, where is
Portia when I need her?

■

I went from house to house for
Kennedy, 1960.

■

Aged four months in small oak
barrels, hint of pork and onions.

■

A golden straw color with
a bright clarity, Iron City.

■

Almost no salt, almost no
sugar—Cribari Brothers.

■

Fermented in new oak barrels
for 40,000 years.

■

Give my regards to Zeno,
remember me to Sigma Square.

■

A hope chest full of rotten
old sheets and pillow cases.

■

Chicago Semite Viennese,
a brown rat from St. Louis.

■

Born-again pie, the sugar
separates the second time.

■

Pope John Paul is not a Christian
according to Pat R.

■

Rue des Rosiers red and
yellow stars Gare Saint Lazare.

■

The monoplane is God
soothing us for half a minute.

■

The trailer, more banking in
less time, I didn't see it.

■

Mas Banca en Menos
Tiempo, the soothing sign says.

■

It's not God after all, it's
the Chase Manhattan Branch Bank.

■

I don't mind the nudists—I
just can't stand the vitamins.

■

Little precious darling dove?
Little darling dove, my ass!

■

Stealing the words right out of
my mouth, you plagiarist.

■

The happiness of the dogs
running into the waters.

■

The monoplanes are still there—
doesn't mean a thing this time.

■

The five flags, Spain, France, Canada
United States, P.R.

■

The dogs barking and carrying
sticks for the poor humans.

■

I lived in America
for eighty, ninety, some years.

■

My own head was small and round,
I was a Mongolian.

■

I deposited an immense
number of eggs and died.

■

Don't leave one child behind, if
it's too slow cut its small throat.

■

Drink Albigensian beer,
eat Confederate matzos.

■

A jackal will eat anything,
he'll eat a dead jackal.

■

Take Andrew Jackson,
murderer of the first order.

■

You're not going to force cheese
down my throat, not this Sunday.

■

Her T-shirt gets tangled
when she turns over in the grass.

■

Her nightgown too, when they lie
down in bed—the second date.

■

Take Theodore Roosevelt,
read his 600 letters.

■

Take Gettysburg, Pennsylvania,
take the Eisenhower years.

■

Always the goyische kopf
doesn't get it—the Joosh joke.

■

I was put here for one reason—
to test *you*, rotten thing.

■

Poor old slumbrous derelict,
stinking feet, stinking hair and beard.

■

Are they stupid enough to
believe they are immortal?

■

The ball was magic, how it
came to him in the bushes.

■

I never said Nero was
worse than Hitler, you said it.

■

Salonika or Vilna, which
do you remember most.

■

How many Dolgapyats
could there have been after the war?

■

Dream is I went from city
to city speaking Yiddish.

■

Remember the one who saved
your life, don't forget my name.

■

I'll be back before you know it,
old almond eye, old tear-drop.

■

One of them gets left for 20
years, one of them forever.

■

I don't want to be either
Nausicaa *or* Penelope.

■

A broken bed at the side
of the road—a Queen I think.

■

Charity is the right foot of
justice—sometimes the knee.

■

There were at least 25
years between the two of them.

■

He was her father's age, maybe
a year or two older.

■

I had a way of letting the fire
rage under the dross.

■

The water-tap is closed suck
some mud it's good for your pipes.

■

The smiling face of
industrial consolidation.

■

I can keep a coal fire
going for seven full days.

■

Watching the honey locust
die a little at a time.

■

They probably would like to bomb
San Juan, not Vieques.

■

Try to keep in mind Nausicaa,
her straw hat and earrings.

■

Her fine white dress, her sandals,
her rings, her ivory headband.

■

Most of all her mule and
the pretty wheels of her carriage.

■

Her height, her passion, her courage,
her humor, her cunning.

■

Decoration Day, Puerto Rico,
year 2002.

■

If somebody yelled "Bingo"
you'd walk a lot faster than that.

■

You're not the only pineapple
on the pineapple bush.

■

Whoever invented wraps they
should drown in salt water.

■

There are a thousand theories
about pit bulls, pro and con.

■

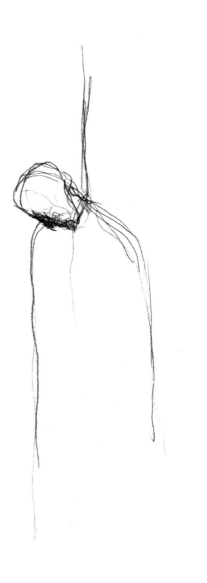

28

To be managed, that is the
most threatening thing of all.

■

No dog ever flogs
another one, you can count on that.

■

Ike Williams carrying his scrapbook
into Dunkin Donuts.

■

Larry Holmes in the
preliminaries, best fighter around.

■

If those two dogs stop projecting
there will be no more war.

■

Wraps are not that bad,
accept the profundity of wraps.

■

A puddle full of crossed
wires—bad communication.

■

Anne Marie has hidden
the Spanish dictionary.

■

Caruso at the Hotel
Carlyle, 1922.

■

Tiso the Slovak, a
Catholic priest and Jew hater.

■

You can eat horse meat but you
can't step on the same dog twice.

■

Now obsess on the wet kiss,
now obsess on the red knife.

■

Making a Christmas tree out
of foreskins, Warsaw, Poland.

■

Bartok at the Bronx zoo
on his way to the polar bears.

■

Keep your hands to yourself, where
do you think we are, in bed?

■

"Ecstasy or some other
dirty word," Rizzo said that.

■

I had a way of shaking
the clinkers to the bottom.

■

Burning coal and sprinkling dust
on top of the fire underneath.

■

Like cats in love, endless
noises, endless sitting there coy.

■

Like cats posturing, some are
kissing, some only fucking.

■

Ruth had all of her white teeth
pulled out and replaced with gold.

■

Saddest underpants I
ever saw—yellow polka dots.

■

He's the more soulful of the
two, sounds like someone crying.

■

Except he lacked love, he was
almost a Jew, Ulysses.

■

Burning bituminous and
loving the stink of blue gas.

■

What about secrecy, what
about not getting published?

■

The way they lived on the roofs,
the hot nights of ecstasy.

■

Monk at the Five Spot, Monk
at the Carlyle, 1965.

■

Between her thighs the odor
of magnolia, smell it!

■

I'm 78, still
alive, waking up every night.

■

Sucking my toes, most boring
and disgusting thing of all.

■

Trilling was just one of my
teachers, I had some good ones.

■

Honor your poet, one of
Moses' shattered commandments.

■

Rebecca, if there is an
afterworld, you will have it.

■

She knew he was a prick but
she wanted to marry him.

■

I caught someone loving his
enemy and turned to stone.

■

Hath not a Jew helicopters,
hath he not bazookas?

■

Dream is I'm in Ruzhin
planting tobacco on the hill.

■

As an iconoclast I am
ready to break your balls.

■

I possess the truth—have a
Chinese pear in the meantime.

■

We stand in awe of you and
your potential, Microsoft.

■

If there was time I'd stop
saying good morning to Zeno.

■

Indeterminacy—walking
up and down my front and back steps.

■

What is it you're not supposed
to feed here, the kangaroos?

■

Fits at night, constant lethargy,
joint pains, diabetes.

■

Dream is I'm in Bialystok
writing my poems in Polish.

■

Hath not an Arab blood,
hath he not his own bazookas?

■

Hath not their own tents, art not
the flaps also eternal?

■

Ist Ariel a sprite, ist
der name not most Kaliban?

■

There's Jesus again, singing
songs that even dogs don't hear.

■

It burns the eyes and the lungs, the
taste of it in the mouth!

■

Hypertension, jitteriness
and general stupor.

■

I will cut my Rose o'Sharon
down, I will destroy it.

■

I could describe it all in
numbers, I even did once.

■

One droll rat after another,
oh Yerushalayim.

■

Look God, look at us sharing
a smoke in Jerusalem.

■

Look God, this Jew and this Arab
in Waterloo Village.

■

Poverty, ignorance, super-
stition, mice—I miss you!

■

He always clung to the melody,
I learned that from him.

■

Yet, what does it mean, what is
it an imitation of?

■

Here comes a genteel one,
sipping his glass of tea!

■

Wires always make love to
each other, amorous wires.

■

The organ has been the downfall
of everything Jewish.

■

Farewell Mandelstam!
Goodbye Stalin, you ugly cockroach!

■

Melancholy, you
prude, I devoted my life to you.

■

Ah, Spanish barber, what was
once one dollar is now twenty.

■

He believed in total
assimilation an anarchist.

■

Rubbing the Russian Sage every
day—seven months a year.

■

How could there be duels with them—
they had no honor to lose.

■

I'll be back before you know
it, little green butterfly.

■

Anne Marie is half-amused
at my stealing her best words.

■

Largest, bluest of all the
birds in my back yard, no song.

■

Walking down I don't count the stairs
as I do when going up.

■

What is more bloodthirsty and
oppressive, God or Country?

■

Ronald Reagan told us we
would have to find our own straw.

■

Eaten by rats still alive
no milk left Rockefeller.

◼

The clay pits on the river,
where we learned about justice.

◼

Reuben and Dan the best
bricks so I picked up a few.

◼

We didn't have any wheels to
push them, we had to drag them.

◼

There was no love from one end
of the Nile to the other.

◼

What do you think we did on
Friday night, go to Temple?

■

Nobody knows our work songs
anymore, nobody sings.

■

Ours was a full eight inches,
forget it, oh Reuben, Benjamin.

■

Every son that is born
you should drown him in the river.

■

What about straw, baby, what
about the twelve-hour day?

■

We had a terrific brick
fight once, everything turned red.

■

I have heard of marble soap
dishes and bars of white soap.

■

There is no difference between
one whip and another.

■

Not much clay on our part of
the river, we used fresh mud.

■

So few understand any
more, I count only seven.

■

48

Reagan met the death squad on
his way to the boiler room.

■

A half grown goose, already
eating weeds, shooting baskets.

■

Leviticus, I am with
you all the way, no ménages.

■

Jimmy Durante, that's a
singer after my own heart.

■

We had knives in our boots,
Luckies and Camels in our mouths.

■

Dream is there's a robin on
my grave for over an hour.

■

The blue flower just
suddenly starts, my overwrought sage.

■

Honeysuckle again, can
you believe how fast it went?

■

Dream is I'm watching a
noisy peacock in my backyard.

■

Dream is his loud scream keeps me
company every morning.

■

You have parsley on your fingers,
potatoes on your toes.

■

I have come to deface the
coinage. Give me a dollar.

■

I'm going to go cut my
own throat right after breakfast.